Canyon

Falls

Canyon Falls

Collected Poems
Volume 4

Richard Gartee

LAKE & EMERALD PUBLICATIONS

Published by Lake and Emerald Publications, LLC
www.lepublications.com

Library of Congress Control Number: 2013917945

Paperback ISBN: 978-0-9895104-7-9

Cover Photo: Richard Gartee

*for muses
old and new*

Contents

Preface

This anthology is principally comprised of poems from two privately issued poetry collections written decades apart. Yet they are united in their observation of that moment when love overtakes us and reasoning faculties flee in the face of it. *Canyon Falls* is not as the cover photo might suggest, about a place in nature, but the image of two distinct metaphors explored in this volume.

Canyons, with or without waterfalls, provide some of the most beautiful vistas to be found in nature. Yet we know a canyon is comprised of sharp jagged rocks, steep ledges, and dangerous footfalls. And, we know its very depths have been carved by the indomitable flow of water.

Isn't there is a moment when we become aware that we are about to fall in love, when the future appears beautiful, like the magnificent view from a canyon's rim? Sometimes we peek over the precipice and step back. Sometimes we jump in feet first anyway, seeking that powerful flow we know is at the canyon's heart.

And that first rush of love? Doesn't it feel like you've ripped open your chest and allowed waves of joy to pour out of your heart like an unstoppable waterfall? But the waterfall is not the kind that gently cascades down a rocky hillside. It's the kind early-spring snowmelt causes to flow hard and fast. Ever widening the passage from which it rushes, pounding away the unyielding rocks below with a roar.

One might say these are poems written by a man, about a man falling in love. I admit that's true. But there is also a study here – of that moment when the breath stops, but the heart races. There is risk in trusting that incomprehensible leap from the canyon edge will result in something good. There is that immersive experience in the midst of pure love energy. There is reflection after the fact. And finally, there is forgetting about the hundred-foot fall the next time we leap into the arms of love. —*Richard Gartee, 2013*

In Cancun

a sandy beach
a small umbrella in your drink

lathered in SPF 15
and still turning red

your bikini
two strings
reflected on your shades

Cancun's blue waves play
beyond my reach

an Irish heart calls
and I respond
from a thousand miles
swimming every stroke.

Waiting on a Wave

Days at the beach which have
no time
all gone without thought
but full of memories

Places and people nearby
who once laughed walking
through skimmer deep water
kicking it with our toes

The now doesn't last
long then it's gone
and it's hard to stay with it
even floating on a wave

A bag of water being moved
by a body of water
in fluid motions of the planet
transiting from continent to continent

In the waiting
in the crest of waves
the movement of this bag of water
by the greater body of water

In the waiting churns the thoughts
like foam after the wave
has hit the shore

Waiting for the feeling of
somewhere other than here
to dissolve into just here

Astronauts laze overhead
looking down,
looking for home,
can't see us
afloat on a wave
watching the waves break down
into component sparkles
of reflected sunlight
and realization that these
reflected bits are
wavelets within the wave.

Panes of French Windows

Driving along
the shore
and imagining I would see
you that evening
I saw your face
in rings of blond curls

When I arrived back at the rented beach house,
it was but dark and empty
only a small vein of light fell through
the front window
So I made up a bed
and was going to sleep
when I heard the knock of a friend
who insisted I get up
that we go out for ice cream
and good company.

A Small boardwalk restaurant
splashed warm yellow light
out French windows and the guitarist
spilled delicate chords out the unpainted door

We walked in and I saw you
sitting up in the rafters
watching the show
suddenly my emotions were flooded
with the thoughts that this fantasy had come true.

when the guitar stopped and it was late,
I ask you to come with me
it seemed somehow all worked out.
we were snuggled in your hotel,
your cool silk

warm against me
then it suddenly didn't.
We each had
something we each saw earlier
but no one knew what to do with it.

The Evening, Thoughts of Your Radiance

The evening, of the day we met
I thought of your radiance.
Radiance
so brilliant, hundreds of steps below me

warmth in your eyes
sparkling like the hot
September second,
sun did
on the rush of sea waves around us.

aura
of your magnetism
speaking something
directly to me

A voice which penetrates my chakras
vibrates them
and energy stirs.

That day I knew you, from somewhere
in our hearts long ago I felt it at once.

My eyes turned to you
I saw you again and again
In my mind's eye

again and again
that climb upward
that slide downward

And some miraculous
workings of this world

found us side by side
eyeing each other

I noticed you noticing,
and saw you
in many shapes I liked

As your warmth came near me
I felt your heat flare
it touched my right arm
from inches away…
just your being near

I turned and you were toward me.
your breasts touching an open door
of warm emptiness
in which fell
(like a vacuum)
the love and thoughts
I carried these last few days.

Sailing Before the Storm

The moon
hid itself for some time
behind a large grey mass
of clouds above and below it
yet from them leaked a wide band of light
giving that section of sky
a glow

Leaving behind the small sands of the beach
and small drives of the mind,
we board a small sloop for a night-long sail
away from the last look I remember in her eyes

I thought the last change
is really at hand, this is such an auspicious sign
having a full moon on your birthday
riding small crests
of turquoise waves
on a dark night.

then lights and shapes
began to shift
and the face of the sphere
began to emerge
a full moon seemed to glow
like a Japanese lantern.
its light was soft
and diffused by veils

shadow of clouds
stratified and became
thin bars of horizontal filter
shading this part and that
I knew what I was seeing

my life emerged from
its cell and become
the light that it was
I could see the process
single pointedly focusing
inwardly on one center
yet merging with everything
external
            with everything that exists,
knowing my own center
yet being everything
in that.

the ocean continued
but the night was bright
white moon light
shining on a deep
deep blue sky
and I was.

First Dance

Her breasts fluttered against me as we danced.

Moon eyed and weak kneed

I held her like a cupped butterfly;

trembled at remembering her touch.

And when she flew away that Sunday

I was sprinkled with the pollen of her wings.

Love Awakens and Lingers

your lips say words
your mouth cannot speak

your laughter rings bells
which open my heart

the stars fall against
cloudy sunsets

we take each step
as each one comes

and night falls
and is gone

your eyes linger into
my sleep
as I lie down

I wake early and taste
your tongue in dream kisses
we've never done

a heart feels your parting
as wings take air into thunder

you are left here
living in my head.

Falling Forward

Falling forward
into your eyes
as we converse
I become immersed
in your being

Sense of your
presence
steals my breath

I tremor from your
attention

Where do I find the
integrity to not
sweep into your life?

I hear your story tell me
that you've just left
a life, as is that
which I already live

And love, a temporary
assuage from the lonely
grind which you say
broke you

I feel your call
to healing
and it takes all the
clarity I can assume
to penetrate the vaporous
perfume of your breath
dancing on my soul.

Ever Presence

I see a woman in a jeep
her fingernails are painted red
my heart leaps, I think of you.

I hear a bird's call in the morning
it reminds me of your laugh
I could hold you in my lap forever
and listen to your breath in my beard.

The mind keeps turning up new thoughts,
and you seem in them all,
like the sound of the beach
in every shell held to the ear.
It's very pleasing to find you
in my life.

Falling Before the Artist

If the age is dawning
Aquarius
it might as well be in your
very blue eyes
that held me in
your aura
thriving on your scent,
feeling, your edges of intuition
fluttering at my heart charka
to see what I was made of.

And the answers I hope you found
to be far different
from imagination I had yesterday
and not
for those thoughts but
knowing not
fueled by visions of peach halves
and impressions of
shapes of woman
and a voyage not
yet embarked into your azure eyes.

Dreams Don't Go

Your face is in my thoughts
then I find you in my dreams
lounging together in recline
laughing, not quite a teasing promise there

Another night, another dream
against all improbability
that we will ever cohabit
the same dream at the same time

Yet you won't go
from my thoughts
from my dreams
I am pulling for you
in the shower, when my thoughts
rush like water
you come in daydreams
like you come in nightly dreams
that don't go away
despite the logic of my left brain
despite the coincidences that never happen
I lie wrapped in sleepy pleasure
my heart yearning, dreams don't go.

Awakening

Fragile delicacy plays
across my mind
in my morning awakening

softness
tastes its way into
that last veil of dreams

dreams which melt
like fog in the dawn
sunlight

the natural feelings
which are expressing themselves
from my sleep belong
like dew on the lawn

smiles in the morning dawn
is the sky
over you in my arms.

Continental Divide

Spring lawns are sprinkled
with yellow chamomile flowers
Magnolias and jasmine have taken me
like a sweet dream with their breath
in the April atmosphere

Me, sitting at the end
of a sand dune in Florida

You, between two mountains
on the western slope of Colorado

We, on a small stone flying
through dark as night sky

Our beings as big as the planet
looking out over the black universe
from this speck of small dust.

Coming to Colorado

I want to pick up the phone
and hear the sound of you
in my ear

I see my future in your
blue eyes
and can hardly wait for
it to arrive

I look at the attraction I have
for you and the thoughts I see
arise

and wonder if it's all right
as I do my best to let these
feelings be just what they are
as they dance by

Closing my eyes, seeing your face
a thousand miles afar
I hold you in my heart
night and day.

Expectations

What expectations have we from afar
as I prepare to fly
and you prepare to meet me
yet we dwell in this stasis
where we don't know each other
in so many ways
yet seem to know each other well.

You close your eyes and
see us holding hands
I close mine, and feel your
nakedness against me
in the dark softness of
your sleigh back bed.

We discuss many topics
and talk for hours
but leave our expectations
unsaid.

I prepare the mind for
acceptance of your every wish
on this our first rendezvous

And you prepare, I don't know
how, but I'm sure with
worry and concern.

each of us, I know, hoping
it is just what it's supposed
to be for the other, hoping
that love has found us out.

On Entering the Canyon

Seeing a picture of the Grand Canyon,
remembering twice being there,
Similarities of both visits could be
defined in three phases of experience.

On first approach, one is amazed by the
sumptuous vista which meets the gaze.

Overwhelmed with the promise of its beauty
one is drawn to the rim.
The power of its potential naturally attracts
one to lean beyond the edge
for a look into the canyon's soul.
The depth of what lies below produces,
with a profound vertigo, the sense
that one is about to fall into vast depths.
It is scary, but one enters in.

Once the journey into this wonder has begun,
each new level, every turn of the trail
deepens the sense of awe.

One discovers that all of the beauty
felt before entering the canyon
was but mirage when compared to the
ever growing wonder experienced
as one pursues its depths.

On Entering the Metaphor

On first approach I am amazed
at the lightness of being given off
by the attraction between our two hearts.
The promise of its beauty draws us to the edge.

The night our first really long phone conversation
occurs, you laugh and ask "What are we doing?"
Through the phone I feel myself looking over
a threshold into your lovely smile.
I answer "I do not know... just sharing,
seeing what becomes."

We experience a relationship, as yet undefined,
as it evolves.
But, speaking strictly for me, in that early time
I felt the fear, of vertigo,
like Butch Cassidy and Sundance holding hands,
about to jump off the cliff.

In a sense, I am immersed in feelings for you.
In another, I am watching myself immersed
and watching this relationship self-create
as we put aside our fear,
and enter,
and go deeper,
it seems to grow in beauty
it seems what was wonderful before
has more potential
and expands its vistas with each turn.

At the start, I was overwhelmed,
but having left the rim and entered in
I have left behind the fear of falling.

Waking Beside You

Waking beside you
I open my eyes
to a softness
shining from your face
as though you are
on another plane.

Your eyes open
and smile sweetly at me
Between us there is
no space, just sharing

between our eyes
a tender dawning
the fever of our love
now subdued
in a mist of romance

In an alabaster light
glowing from within you,
like a deer in the road
I am dazed by
the experience.

Your lips as soft as
buttercups
your body lithe as dance,
we lie in fragrance
of flowers growing
from our hearts
whose petals are the
caresses our fingertips
have lightly strewn
over the landscape of
our flesh.

While we traverse wild
fields of emotions
time hangs suspended.
And honored to be
in love
I am honored to
be loved by you
every moment a jewel
to be treasured
movement refracted
in the radiance of
each second, precious.

I am filled with you
to overflowing and
when it comes time for
departing no yearning
tears, no longing,
I am comforted and
satiated and with your
presence, enchanted.

what grace has on us
unfolded
the blessing
of this,
together.

A Day of Parting

A silver plane flies
past a full moon
I think of you
You'll be landing soon

It's such a great day
to be flying
It's been a day that
breaks a face with smiling

And it's a night
bright with moonlight
And the muse which
was lost has found me.

Last Night

Holding you in my heart
felt like a warm cup of soup
held in my palms
as we talked
and the last summer rain fell
on the first fall leaves
carpeting the walkway
outside our window

laughter
tangled in your blond curls
and honesty shined
outside your brown skin
as we spooned fragrant
thick yellow stew
into our mouths
and shared rare spaces

what makes me feel I have known you
for so long and so far?
It is like the room I make for you
in my heart
with comfortable chairs,
burgundy rugs and
warm incense
that beckons you to stay
for a while in my own love.

Just Watching

I'm drinking tea from a
cup that says San Francisco
thinking about a woman
in Colorado
and watching the energy in
my heart flow
as she laughs
or answers
or doesn't answer

I know
I should let it go
but it pulls strong and we talk so long
yet we watch
as it unfolds

she says good-bye
I close my eyes
and sleep 'til dawn
in love with her.

Facing self

this attraction for you
becomes desire, wants & need
i know the questions, but
i am looking for the question,
which when ask, will set me free

it is yearning
it is pulling
it is hurting
it is tearing from my heart

if i have ever thought
i've passed beyond all that,
here it sits in the center
of space
looking me square on
presenting moment by moment
opportunities to deal with it.

Facing self II

What karmic seeds are sown
1500 miles away
with a card, a call, a thought
watch it dance away
watch the mind creating plans
as the heart reaches out with
both hands
to take what it feels it needs
and all the while I
try to stay seated in a place
of consciousness
but even though I watch,
it still happens.

The Muse Is Back

The muse is back
and I welcome her
with open arms and
full rejoicing

I dance her lyrics
across a page
acknowledge the pain
which I've hidden so long

From her absence I
have run
now she returns I lend
myself
to her will

In her presence my heart
like cocoa butter
in summer melts
yielding intoxicating
chocolate essence

Her thoughts an
aroma of similes
in my mind.

If You Could Keep On Singing

if you could keep on singing
i could write all night
on darkened streets with flashing lights
i hear your melody

and the words flow with your promise
to be the singer of my songs

then when it has ended
i'm not sure how to stop
for it is those rhythms
i remember
from the times that you were hot

like a comma,
in my sentence
your changes are no more than a pause
while the sense of their feeling
moves my very soul
like thoughts in gestalt flashes
a continuity of spaces
implies the whole

not your voice
not driving rhythm
not intensity
or your sexual thrusts
but a whole becoming
materialized before we die.

Forgiveness II

When the heart is flowing love
she forgives herself
trespasses
minor and major
as though they were small
yellow chamomile flowers
spread throughout the grass
in fields of her lives.

As a Gift, A Blessing

Dogwoods are in flower
and they line the road

I sing your name
as I go along it

With its sound
I see your face,
your smile,
and make up constant scenarios

she is in the mountains
and we are picking flowers
which fall at our
feet with warmth
and affection

we sink to the soft grass,
spread our blanket
on the meadow

the more I relax the
deeper you touch me
Encompassed by a cloud
of warmth, I am
drowned in the
sweet vapors of it

soft caresses of
pink flowers and
your laughter over my ears
your smile over my eyes
your dance against my body
and your light
with my own

I don't know why I feel
this way

Some breeze stirs me from
deep inside
Like a flag moves I salute you
and fly away on dreams

Sweet sleep
in which you kiss me

and I open my mouth
your tongue enters
with a taste of warmth
I dream on

Morning lights my eyes
I wake aglow
with memories of dream lovin'

A full circle comes
A poem twenty years past
comes to mind
first love long beyond
yet with you, renewed
in tentative first sweet kisses

In the temple of my heart
a goddess comes to visit
Overwhelmed, I offer petals
of devotion
I serve her food and
myself am fed with the nectar
of her attention

she draws from me my best
and I offer it to her

she makes of me a reed
and I allow her to flow
through me

becoming a whisper behind
every thought
an elemental muse
of directed self-exploration,
a destination for every
step toward a pinnacle

A few moments with you
renews
my love dances in me long
after time spent together is passed

I thank the goddess
for this brief experience
with you,
for filling my life and thoughts
with your every move.

Mind & Heart

I once wrote:
The mind
is a small
place to live

but now my heart
is a mansion
illuminated by
your light.

Reclined In a Love Light

I want to write a poem about you
about how you look when you're sleeping
when your eyes open and you're just peeping
with the softest look.

We're lying in bed together
I open my eyes in the early dawn
Looking across the pillow at you
you slowly come awake
your eyes are so soft
your heart is so full
love is overflowing out of your eyes

You are reclined in a love light
there a soft glow,
from light, slightly defused
Your lips are luscious to me
I never want to move
I want to just lie there with you

There is no doubt about love
our love is there and it's real
just the look in your eyes
says it's something you feel
The way you look touches me,
causes me to melt.

Crystal Blue of Your Eyes

The crystal blue of your eyes
feeling truth,
leads me into your heart
without hesitation

No one knows where we go
when we are alone
but with you
we go into love.

Love IV

Love is in an endless supply
flowing spontaneously
from a source
within

It cannot be
created, destroyed
halted, or stopped

It can
on any given day
be ignored
forgotten
making it seem to disappear

But love is a force
to be reckoned with
when of its own accord
it rises
and bursts forth and out
a new channel
to a new beat
of a renewed heart.

A Little Good

A little romance in my life
does me good
a glow of good wine
with dinner
is like a winter romance
with you

A little dance is good
in my life
like a brisk morning
mountain climb
A little rock and roll
stirs my heart
shakes my soul awake

A little press of your
body to mine
awakens nerves
hibernating in the dermis
beneath my body hairs

A little touch of you
in my life does me good.

Destiny

Lie back on the chaise lounge
looking up at a sky alive
with stars, dusted
like confectioners' sugar

Looking for a sign
you see a shooting star
You ask is this really it?
and you see another

you say to yourself
if you see just one more
you'll be sure
and a dozen stars leap from heaven
It's your destiny, it's your life.

Destiny, who leads you like a child
taking your finger and pulling you
by the hand to what she wants
to show you

Destiny, who has a purpose
taking stars from the sky and
putting them where they need to land

Destiny who has unfolded you
and unfolded me
into each other's arms.

The Rain Wet Grass

The rain wet grass on the edge of the road
the damp bliss of a perfect rain
wild love and wild times on a perfect day

I love you so much it hurts
and you really feel it
you turn to me and say
"remember this day,
it was a day of perfection."
It was July fourteenth.

October Twelfth

The moon sphere was so
huge it blocked the road
two lanes wide at the horizon

The plume of last night's space shot was
hued in orange and yellow
I watched the rocket engine burn
A white hot fiery point of light
like the brightest star
speeding through the sky

Then she called
at half before midnight
full of talk about God
and mountain cabin dreams
and probably more than a little wine

What does this phenomenon of lights
and moons like large orange Japanese lanterns
bring, but memories
of other October days, since past.

Unimportant Things

Did it have to come to this
that out of meeting
we meet our means
and feel we have to
go on with it?

did it have to come to this
to make me realize
that change must go on

I only weep for you
like a brush
bleeds for inspiration
on a blue-sky day

but did it have to
come to this
before I'd realize
how easy it would be
to do it your way

I can't believe we
ever thought it important
to lose our way.

Divine Sister

There is a place in me
which feels like a peach pit
or a cherry stone
when I deal with you

But the answers do not seem
to spring from it, like saplings
from the seed

Yet it
finds my own self
when I ask for our motivations

When something is unresolved between us
it is as though
there were a stone sitting on my heart
weighing on us
heavy and unborn.

When I talk to you on the phone
I hear the difference in my tone
and how different we have become
since we last talked
our hearts still beat as one
I in you, and you in me
one being, ever free

But as you spoke out so plainly
I could see we had two different views
We were living within our hearts
My firm intention is to pass
through each confrontation in this world
like it has no substance and can harm nothing real

I bless you
with the love of God
which I would share with the world
but with you
I have to keep relearning the joyous lesson
that there is no love but God's
and yours and mine and everyone else's
No love
but love
and that it's so imperative to see
in each other
the divine
          despite all appearance to the contrary.

Seeing Her Anew

Warmth in her eyes
and God in her heart
draws Everything from me
with a smile

She calls me intense
and abhors her own prejudice
but in my humblest vision
she is the highest being

my heart races slightly
as I leave meditation
and drive to her house

the children are dancing their way
in and out of their bedtimes
and she is still moving
at the same pace I saw
hours before.
I am pleased by her power.

and watching my own self
I settle in to wait for the
dialogue which will take us within
it courses its way through
my week-end to hers
all one God to hers.

Winter

Starring out French windows
at a garden covered in winter frost
a glass of merlot in my hand
while warmth of the heat blasts at my feet
warmth of the wine ages my mind

Mellowed I walk out into the scent
of the cold, the bite of the air

From speakers hidden in the soffits
so the songs seem to float in from nowhere
female voices from the rafters command me
to have a merry little Christmas

Thoughts of you interlude
with thoughts of Paris next year
Maybe it is the merlot or maybe
a vision
who knows? At this point it's indistinguishable

With poinsettias of red and white
at hand everywhere
except through French doors
of snow frosted gardens.

Krishna Blue Eyes

Someone told me this was Krishna's birthday
and I laughed because I thought of you the whole day

I thought of your lotus feet
and your perfect service

I thought of the bhakti,
the young devotee of pure love
I met one day in a busy fair
selling magazines with your picture
doing anything she could for you and
opening hearts with the transcendental love
in those blue eyes

Years later I saw her again
we were standing by a cash register in a health food
restaurant and she was counting change
making money with some concentration
I saw the lines on her face
where she had folded her sari and put it away for a
worldly life
of husbands and babies,
separations and responsibilities

yet as I looked at the worn places
where the world changed her and marked her
she looked up
and in her eyes
your blue form shone.

Stirred and Shaken

She stirred me
like I haven't been shaken in a while.
Beauty a beam of light in a smile,
hip-hugging long bell bottoms
that shifted so seductively
that in her ordinary walk
I imagined silk skirts made of veils
on a belly dancer's hips,
imagined her round breasts
in a bikini top.
I noticed myself looking for her all night long.

One Heart

The sky freckled
with white stars
and jeweled with
a full moon of
your lotus feet

Ken said one could feel
your willingness to be here
feel the sense of your closeness
in the midnight air at the lakeside

how open your heart
your eyes
your mouth
bestowing your every blessing
with your slightest move

how long we have been one heart
without ever knowing the sweet, sweet, essence
between us
I feel initiated by your divine presence,
ready to flow at a moment's inspiration.

Pathway of Light

Thinking of trying again
brings me ready for you.

I know how I would like things to be
and am ready to enfold their differences
in one pathway of light
that illuminates as we proceed
in the right direction.

Soft Appeal

The soft appeal of shy eyes
and gentle curves
sweep over my entire being
into thoughts of her
The sweet scent of a gardenia
she brought in the afternoon
still emanates from the vase
and fills the house
tickling my nostrils
with memories and foolish fantasies

The soft contact of our bodies
while posing for photos
a brush of my cheek when
saying good-bye
combine in my mind
causing my heart to quicken

The soft touch of her hand
lingers in my fingertips
I reciprocate with casual affirmations
and ask myself if she is flirting
Culture, age, and experiential differences
make it difficult to read the navigable
ways through the reedy pond of feelings

The soft shapes of round breasts
round face and belly
obscure the sharp edges of common sense
Awash in a sea of senses
that create waves of feelings
like tides softening the beach sand
I don't know if it is mutual or not
I don't know if it is foolish or not

I don't know if it should come or not
But I do know the damaged heart
is not too hardened to be pried apart
by gentle fantasies.

In Anticipation of You

I awake in anticipation of you
I shower and thoughts of you
run from my mind
like rivulets of water off my arms
The conversations we have
Oh! the conversations we have
run through my imagination
as I soap and rinse and dry

My morning coffee tastes like
memories of the evening before
Its rich aroma awakens me
to a new day of anticipating you

The days between seeing you
flow almost unnoticed
for they are but intervals
in thinking about you
punctuated by phone calls
to make other plans

Throughout these times away from you
a plethora of past and future
lovers enter my life
I notice how strangely
I am behaving
—holding off commitments
—making holes in my schedule
—leaving the door open
in anticipation of you

In someone else the waiting
might be yearning or anxiety
but for me I luxuriate in its sweetness
the unexpected, expected

And I think of the Passover
when a cup is poured
and the door is left ajar
for the coming of Elijah.
Whether the prophet manifests or not
the door was opened
the hosts were waiting
the anticipation of the hoped for
coming.

Something In the Air

Love passes into my fingers
like heat from your palm,
trickles thread like, up my arm
and ties us neatly in knots.

Something else is hanging in the air,
we both are feeling it,
I can tell;
trying so hard not to become involved.

Almost crossing the line
where everything changes
we embrace and part
but in twenty minutes
the phone rings,
you say "tonight was fun."
But isn't there something else,
not quite said, but felt
between the words?

You are all feelings
and I am all thoughts,
but disciplined, focused thoughts
…until I started seeing you.

Now you are much on my mind
and the days between seeing you
are all about seeing you.

Memories of that moment when
something passed between us
and I recollect, for my part
feeling, thinking, worrying that
I am falling a little bit in love with you.

In the interval I notice you have opened a gaping hole
in my chest,
a hole where love exists again
and as it has been written, love hurts.

A sweet pain, thinking of you these days,
but still a real feeling
when my heart hurts
at what should not be happening between us
cannot be.
And reasoning my best
that if this is love
and I love you as I think I do
then I should want what is best for the beloved
not for myself.

I am too afraid that I have
brought you into my disaster
and that if I am sensing
love from you then I must find a way
neither to break your heart
nor give in
to passions
that flood our thoughts

In the natural course of plans already made
I am going away
On the one hand I want to see you
as much as possible before I go
On the other hand must tread so lightly
as not to step on the world's toes
There is real danger here.

I may be reflecting a character in my novel
but you are not a fictional girl
nor is she written about you.

In the morning I pick you up.
Rain threatens
but does not come.

We dive in cool waters of reason
but when we talk
you confess an intensity
that yearns for release.
Our passion is stymied
by a line we cannot break.
I agree. I say I feel the same.
We vow not to go there
and transform our passion into affection.

You don't want to go
and I don't want you to leave
You hold my arm and softly stroke fine hairs
as Shakespeare plays out a tragedy of love lost
and like his two ill-fated lovers
we will never be
and therefore must refine
what we have
into something we define
on another plane
that which we never share
on this one.

Almost

You say, "Let's just make out,"
and you are so near to getting your wish
I want what you want,
feel the intensity you feel.
I hold you against me
our bodies touching every part;
my maleness pulses with blood,
growing with your yearning,
we breathe in and out,
transmuting the energy up,
but again and again it falls
as concentration fails,
and thoughts go to the feelings
of lovers' embrace.

Two would be lovers, trying to behave
and wanting to do everything else instead.
But the prognosis is clear,
from kiss to making out, to making love,
what then? Deniability gone,
fire on the mountain,
great streams of wrath
all the result of failing to maintain
the distance we both hate to keep,
yet keep we must, to keep safe
from much fury.

You steal a kiss from my neck,
you hold your head against me, just so,
just where the slightest suggestion
of movement from me
will put our hungry mouths against each other.
It would be so easy.
Just a brush of our cheeks passing

toward each other's lips
and our tongues would dance.

Your breasts softly against me
make me want to get hard.
I try to find a place of softness
like the afterglow of post coitus.
Can we enjoy the feelings as though
we had when we haven't?
Can I make you something
besides frustrated?

We aren't concentrating on transmuting the energy,
we're busy thinking of the one we're holding
until it seems there can be no going further
without going too far.

Still longing, we are gentle
in our parting,
throwing each other kisses
from a distance;
not the kind of kisses you wanted,
but kisses that are full of love

You go dancing
and I go dining
and drink too much wine

I look at my phone and see
I've missed your call.
I call you back,
you call me back,
and we talk,
speaking one set of words
while feeling another.
We stay on the phone through long pauses,
spacey sweet nothings,

this is real boyfriend girlfriend stuff.

You're calling from your car
waiting to drive
I feel like you want to come.
Are you waiting for me to suggest it?
I feel it so strongly I am sure of it.
There is real danger here.
I am lying in bed naked
talking to you on the phone
in a dreamy romantic haze
with enough wine in me
to weaken my resolve.
It would be too easy
for you to just show up
and have your way with me.
But what then? What of the morrow
when I fly away
and leave you to your thoughts and feelings,
spinning hope and dreams and twice the pain
from having, but also having to hide it?

You're not alone in this
I keep saying
I feel it too

I admit I've found love in you,
but I have to hope you won't be hurt by it
for if you were, what kind of love would that be?

Something of You Lingers

Something soothes me
in your call that makes me
not want to let you go.
I have no ideas,
just feelings,
just breathing,
just being.

It may always be now
as I have often told you,
but the feeling of you lingers
in whatever pulses occur in life
between the moments we talk
and your next call.

The Brush of Lips

At last it's come to this, a brush of lips
and the shakti crackles with our kiss
we both experience the rush of bliss
that lasts and lingers and bespeaks our failures
at being so good with each other's morals
and while nothing we have ever done is wrong
we are surely two mature adults
making more steady progress toward sex than two
determined teenagers ever do

And do you think it will take two years
to lay this monk, or shall he,
holed up in his upper mind,
overlook the fact that you are precisely
the find he has had hid
in some dreamy distant desires
which surface, as you express your needs?

And you lay your head against his lap
in perfect faith
that he has promised to control the situation

yet when he stands by the door to depart
your lips brush and dance away
the first time in a dozen years
and know damn well there's more to come
stirred by your insistent love.

Love V

What is love?
puzzled the poet
as he struggled
with his couplets

What is love?
mused the artist
as she dabbed
her colors on paper

Love, Love,
"Love is all you need,"
crooned the Beatles
in their chorus

How do I get more?
cries the child
inside us

"Love springs
spontaneously
from within,"
the avatar advises

Love is an eternal moment
existing only in the
always now
observes the sage

"Stop," said the mind,
"there are too many
conflicting opinions.
Tell me, oh heart,
what is love?"

What is love,
is the question.
the heart would have
liked to answer

But the enraptured heart
cannot speak
it only sighs
aaaaa, ahaaa, ahhhhh

For in the heart,
love is,
Love just is

Love is a
watershed moment
when your heart floods
and yourself is washed away

For me,
love is an
ever renewing flow
of energy
through my heart
…for you.

Here — now

Here – now, the ideal truth

of what is reality.

Yet my misbehaving mind

dances with thoughts of you

tho you are not here

and then is now –now.

Initiation

When the time comes
it grows late
I have made my confessions
we have touched hands
and know the warmth in two beings of God

I feel at hand the timing
I have waited for since the first moment of today

I rise
and turn off the light
It is not dark
there are lights from the other rooms
and hall
we talk a bit more and I suggest
we sit.
She moves toward me slightly and begins
to be nervous
I close her eyes
and focus her breath

We are one being
floating on inhalation
of breath rising and falling
on one small planet
in one unified field
creation

Imagining the breath
flowing into and out of the heart
it becomes a luminescent
cloud of light encircling us.

It expands and surrounds us
until the ecstasy
astounds us
at last
it has really found us.
As the sound of the breath
is passed.

Listening to the words the mind forms
when hearing the breath moving;
slowly inhale,
the noise seems to say to the mind s-o-o-o-o
Exhale and the sound is like h-a-u-m-m-m-m
So and Haum
So and Haum
speaking within you
by its movements
the mind becomes occupied by these two sounds
It becomes calm.

God consciousness begins
to vibrate in my pituitary
my arm begins to tremble
my hand
on her eyes and head
for the blessing.

We finish and pray deeply,
personally,
intuitively,
we feel the answer come
and it is a struggle to open the eyes
this was the offering I
have been waiting to share.

My bare feet
dance across the cool
water on the fall grass lawn
as I leave

She will sleep better than she has
in a long time
and I shall probably need little sleep at all
so awakening, the experience
of initiation.

The Other Side of Night

The other side of night
where blackness remains,
but just ahead, dark is making
preparations to flee.

Spent is the earlier side of night,
when two tumbled into bed
wide awake in wanting
kissing like sleep wasn't coming.

Now it is the other side of night,
where sweet dreaming
blossoms into reawakening
and dream like bliss making.

The side of night
far enough from morning
that love is all the warmth you need
and the room is filled
with soft after passion breathing
and whispered oblations to each other.

Up the Mountain

Scouting the plaza too many Friday nights
searching for a glimpse of the man
your mother disapproves of

Standing on a Wyoming mountaintop
searching for a signal
Raise your cell phone to the sky
looking for a bar or two
hoping to get a message to him

Summer's gone, you come back home
there he is with your friends
asking who you are.
Being clever you answer
"Who am I?"
but isn't that what we all
really want to know?

You meet to explore that question
and far beyond, explore each other.

Then one day, you say
you can't live your mother's life.
That is true.
But what does that statement really mean to you?

Pleasure flows from the tips of his fingers.
His phallus fills her yearning
Her loving fills to overflowing
Yet something makes you stay away
Leaving him to wonder
why you climbed that mountain.

Parting

The parting of the days
concludes in a parting of the ways
on a night much anticipated
full of fantasies played out in every direction
but your reasonable conclusion
that some distance has given you
that this can't go,
therefore we should not proceed
to confuse our feelings any further,
leaves me nowhere to go
but to acquiesce

You are so clear in your maternal fear
you know what is right for us
I am back where you were weeks ago
and have been lost in your spacey dream
state of my own
but all about you
not from you
but on my own

softness pervades the space
as I offer final instructive guidance
I also offer final blessings
benedictions in a touch
melting between us becomes
a kiss we never shared
comes against our cheeks

I say if you change your mind
fear not to say you want to see me

I hold up both palms
you drive away.

Things to Remember

1. Be at peace wherever you are
for that *is* where you are,
and then you are not looking for peace elsewhere

2. Be happy, right now
for that is the only time there is.
Do not wait to be happy in the future,
for you are always in the now,
never in the future.

3. Love
for that is what you are.
When you let go of the stuff that is between you and
love,
your love will flow like it should,
for that is your true nature.

Letting Go

Letting go
is not so easy
as getting attached

Good-bye to all that
softness
sweet embraces
fantasy
of kisses

Attachment is as easy
as letting the thoughts
roll around in your mind
like loose marbles
expanding
those little thought balloons
you see in cartoons

Letting go
is hindered by those
hills of rolling thoughts
cascading down
one from the other
all about you and me
and never be

Being done
is not being gone
from my mind

My heart feels hollow
There was an opening
made there by you
for you

and now
exists a vacuum
from our parting

It's hard to let go of a vacuum.

Interlude With an Angel

The briefest time that it takes
to breathe in, to breathe out,
for energy to rise, to fall,
these were the moments we shared.

Raising our eyes upward
bringing our energy to our hearts
and our hearts opened.

You entered mine
and pulled me into you.

Our time so brief,
in retrospect, seems fragile,
but in the state of now
you were more than
a fulfillment, a treasure,
a bit of consciousness
in a precious space.
My brief interlude
with an angel.

Here

Here,

I am more aware of stillness

And when it is absent.

Thinking of you

I send many blessings your way.

Beyond the Mind's Small Place to Live

There are many places to live
besides the mind

The world,
Zen experiences of a sunset,
or a tree.
You can live in the world.

Body,
experiences of
extreme pain or pleasure
have taken us from the mind
and focused awareness to the body.

Heart,
strong experiences of love
or hurt
have taken us out of our mind
and into the heart;
have they not?

Consciousness,
when you change your seat
of awareness
to sit in consciousness
and just watch the mind.

So we have all these other places
to live
instead of the mind
but we have not
because we care
what the mind is saying.

As long as we care
what it is saying
we will not leave it.

Just take a giant step back
and watch the mind
From there you will
not have so much care.

Canyon Memories

The old saw is to look before you leap
Sometimes you peek over the precipice
and step back
then someone takes you by the hand
and you jump in feet first anyway

Sometimes you break your bones
Sometimes you break your heart
Sometimes you catch an updraft
and gently fall through a shower of rose petals

In any case, time passes
Your mind revises the experience
And sooner or later you find yourself on the rim
looking over a beautiful vista
You feel someone's soft fingers interlace yours
and as your feet leave the ledge
sharp stones forgotten,
you're hoping for more rose petals.

Watching Waves

Collected Poems Volume 3

in paperback and e-book

ISBN: 978-0-9895104-5-5

Watching Waves is a collection of poems comprised almost entirely of deeply personal interior musings about the nature of reality. Over eighty percent of this collection has never appeared in print before. Themes of a universal God and our search for God are prevalent throughout. Diverse influences of Indian Gurus, Tibetan Lamas, Lao Tzu, Zen, Sufi and Christian mystics inform the book's cosmology

About Lancelot's Grail

New age teachings on self-awareness and enlightenment are explored in an Arthurian-age story of two siblings' journey to enlightenment after they discover Sir Lancelot living as a hermit and uncover his knowledge of the Holy Grail.

Sir Lancelot, abandoned by his once-adoring public, has found enlightenment while living as a hermit.

Sir Bedivere, desolate over the knights' abandonment of the Round Table after the fall of Camelot, has come up with a plan.

Alura and Frith, abandoned at an abbey as children, have grown up in social isolation and are desperate for a new life.

Their lives converge when Frith leads Sir Bedivere to Lancelot's hermitage. There, they learn that Lancelot has found the Holy Grail – within himself. Bedivere tries, without success, to persuade Lancelot to come help him rebuild the Knights of The Round Table. After Bedivere departs, Frith begs Lancelot to teach him, hoping to become a knight. Soon Alura joins them, hoping to snare herself a husband.

Lancelot, torn between a desire to be left alone and an obligation to pass his knowledge on, agrees to teach them, but soon realizes that everyone simply wants to use him. Yet, seeing the spark of awareness growing in Alura and Frith, he persists and leads them on a quest to penetrate the barriers in themselves that keep them from attaining the Grail.

Then Alura falls in love with Lancelot and incites an angry mob. Bedivere urges Lancelot to flee, but Lancelot stays, struggling to finish his work with Alura and Frith in the little time he has left.

Under Lancelot's tutelage Alura and Frith come of age, but the ideas presented in Lancelot's Grail invite the reader to reconsider what coming of age really means.

About Lancelot's Disciple

Frith and Alura are brother and sister who discovered Sir Lancelot living as a hermit in *Lancelot's Grail*. Together they uncovered his knowledge of the Holy Grail, and trained as his disciples. Now their story continues in this compelling sequel.

When Lancelot's spiritual mantel consecrates Alura, Frith is left wondering why the same didn't happen to him. As she becomes established in her seat of Self, Frith resigns himself to remain at the abbey and watch over his sister.

Then, Jacob, a Jewish merchant sent by their father, comes to take Frith on a journey along the ancient Silk Road. A reluctant Frith leaves the Christian abbey he has always called home to sail with Jacob to the Mediterranean city of Tyre.

With four knights for protection, the men caravan to Samarkand, the Central Asian capital of the silk trade. There they meet the Sultan, a wealthy collector of Oriental holy men.

Frith is invited to study at the Sultan's newly formed mystery school, where he is tutored by a Taoist, a Buddhist, and a Hindu Swami. Overwhelmed by metaphysical experiences he receives from them, Frith becomes nearly catatonic during the journey home, causing Jacob to consider revealing hidden Jewish mysticism to set Frith right.

Once back in Britain, Frith must sort out his confusion, attain the Holy Grail, and reconnect with his saintly sister waiting at the abbey.

Read a Sample Chapter from

LANCELOT'S GRAIL

Chapter 1

The August sun burned pleasant, evaporating any memory of the dark years. The sun was gold, the lawns were green and all the abbey gardens were abundant.

Alura was gathering rosemary and shallots in the herb garden near the Abbot's kitchen. She noticed her brother Frith crossing the distant vegetable gardens. He seemed to be playfully following the path of a sunbeam that capered in rhythm to the sway of tall trees. Where it veered from the walkway into the garden he ran after it, performing gawky leaps over the rows of vegetables.

Monks hoeing the beans and peas kept their eyes on the plants and pretended not to see that he crossed their rows instead of following the longer path around. Alura laughed. Frith had been the Abbot's personal attendant since he was a child and had a habit of doing whatever he wanted. Although he was grown now, the monks still indulged him.

Frith was making his way toward the Abbot's kitchen, where Alura had worked since her own childhood. Although the Abbey of St. Benignus wasn't a mixed house – all of the monastics were male – women were employed in the kitchens as cooks, bakers, and chefs. Assisted by younger monks, they prepared magnificent banquets and sumptuous feasts for the Abbot's guests. All but one of the women were married and lived in the nearby village – only Alura was single. She lived on the abbey grounds in a converted storeroom.

St. Benignus was located not far off the old Roman road. A small village with a market and a few tradesmen had grown around it. Travelers would stable their animals at the livery, and then inevitably ask where they could secure a meal and a night's sleep. The liveryman would shrug and point them toward the abbey.

Alura oft heard the Abbot say he wasn't in the business of running an inn; he was busy running a house of God. But safe places to take refuge along the road being rare, he thought it his Christian duty to offer accommodation to those who sought it.

Alura turned back to her task. She was pulling a few more shallots when Frith dashed up and pinched her. Alura emitted a startled squeal and whirled to slap him, but Frith caught her wrist in his hand and kissed her lightly on the cheek.

Alura glanced around quickly before embracing him. "Hello, little brother."

"Not so little; I am now taller than you."

"And none the wiser for it. Suppose someone had seen you do that."

"Well you do it to me."

"Not when anyone might see. I suppose you've come to tell me about the knight?"

"Knight! What knight?"

"The liveryman's wife says a knight has come, all bright and shiny in polished armor. The knight has left him care of a handsome steed."

"And is the knight handsome as well?"

Alura dimpled. "I haven't seen him."

"But you will."

"Oh yes! I'll arrange to be in the dining hall when the Abbot brings him to sup."

"What if he's married?"

"What if he's not?"

Just then Ethelburg, one of the kitchen ladies, poked her head out of the door. "Alura!"

Alura turned and held up her basket, "Just gathering shallots and herbs for the morrow."

"Is that Frith with you?"

"She has poor eyes," Frith said. "Tell her no."

"He has just come," Alura said.

"Frith!" Ethelburg said, "The Abbot is looking for you."

"I have finished my duties for the day," Frith said.

"That may be, but he wants you back."

Touching Alura's sleeve, Frith said, "Let me see what he wants. I will return as soon as I may."

"Don't hurry. I have to finish preparing supper before they will let me free."

"Frith!" Ethelburg called. "It's not tomorrow he wants you. It's now!"

Frith walked toward the building. "Coming, Madame."

"Wait, for me," Alura said.

Alura and Frith entered the Abbot's kitchen. Its tall conical ceiling, open at the top, provided a draft that kept three fireplaces blazing. The monks had a separate kitchen, similar in design, but smaller. This kitchen was dedicated to provisioning the Abbot's more important guests. The Abbot deemed it only fitting to provide richer hospitality to the noble guests who came to the abbey. They, in turn, filled its coffers with their generous donations and the abbey had become enormously wealthy.

Even if Alura hadn't known about the knight, the activity in the kitchen would have told her there was an important guest. There was venison roasting on one fireplace, a pig on the spit of another and several chickens in a great pot of vegetables on the third. All of this was to please the Abbot's guests. The monks lived a more frugal existence. They ate one meal a day, except during Easter. Each monk got bread, soup, two cooked dishes of beans or eggs, cheese and plenty of vegetables.

Frith snatched a sliver of meat off one of the carving tables and popped it into his mouth. The cook waved her cleaver at him.

"I moved here for the ample food," Frith said, grinning.

"You'd make a poor monk."

"I would never be a monk. I couldn't work around all this delicious smelling meat and have to eat a plain diet of vegetables."

"You'd eat well enough," the cook said. "Your sister would see to that."

Alura smiled at their banter. Her brother liked to joke that he sampled all the dishes to make sure the Abbot wasn't poisoned. The Abbot also imported a good wine. Frith sampled that as well.

"Besides," Frith said, "father sent us to the Abbot for jobs, not renunciation."

That was true. Back in the dark years, she and Frith were brought by an elder brother carrying a letter to the Abbot from their father. Their father in better times had contributed substantially to the church. He might yet again when better times returned. Thus Frith and Alura were not treated as novices, but as employees much in the Abbot's favor.

She remembered how hopelessly lost she had felt entering the gates of St. Benignus. She had seldom been off her father's estate and never to a church as large and impressive as this. The family said they were not abandoning them. They said St. Benignus was an important church. That meant they would live in a good moral environment, have plenty of food, and be safe from harm within its walled grounds. From her perspective, her older brothers and sisters had simply decided to get rid of the two youngest siblings. Her proof was that when better times returned, the family did not retrieve them. Further, she felt shocked and betrayed when she learned that there was no money left for a dowry, and thus no opportunity for her to get a husband.

The only bright spot in this crisis was that her best friend and playmate, Frith, was going to be with her. Alura had been one year old when Frith was born, and they had been constant companions from the time they were toddlers.

At first, Alura was given the scut work – gather vegetables from the gardens, fetch water, wash the vegetables, and feed the scraps to the chickens. These jobs, at least, gave her plenty of chances to run out of the kitchen and about the abbey grounds with Frith. That kept her loneliness at bay.

Eventually the two of them were given more responsibilities, but still they managed to finish each day with time to spend together. Over the years Alura learned to be a good cook. It was said she could turn out a tasty dish from whatever God provided, a skill that suited the Abbot's frugal nature very well.

In a sense, the abbey life was good. There was always plenty to eat, which was a blessing itself. Even better, the abbey was a main stopping point for travelers from far places. There were interesting overnight guests and interesting conversations for a girl to listen in on. She was intelligent, bright, and had a good mind, although she had learned that was not a desirable attribute for a woman in search of a spouse.

Alura believed Frith's lot was easier because the consequences of their abandonment seemed more severe for her than for him. Although she sometimes felt like women were chattel, sold for a dowry, bought for power, or to service a husband, the meaning of a girl's life was marriage. Wasn't it? By her age Mother had married and birthed her older brothers.

If only she had been returned to Father's estate... But no, she was stuck at the abbey and it seemed nobody back home was championing her cause. If she was to marry, she must do it on her own.

Read additional chapters and more about both novels at:

www.LancelotsGrail.com

Made in the USA
Monee, IL
07 July 2026